# TABLE OF CONTENTS

*Note: The numbered Wisdom Keys of Dr. Murdock are noted as WKMM#*

**101 The Most Memorable Day of My Life Was In 1994.** If you were to ask me, "What is the most memorable day of your life?"...I call it the greatest day of my life, I would tell you July 13, 1994.

*It happened on a Wednesday morning at 7:00 a.m.*

*It was the day I fell in love with the Person of The Holy Spirit.*

*The Holy Spirit Is The Only Person Capable of Being Completely Satisfied With You* (WKMM#141).

Nobody else is capable of being completely contented with you. He *knows* what is in you...and He *knows* what is not. He *gives* you the most and *requires* the least. He *makes* the greatest deposit.

The Holy Spirit is a *Person.* He is to us what Jesus was to the 12 disciples. What Jesus is to your salvation The Holy Spirit is to your prayer life.

He is not wind. He *moves* like wind.

His entry into a room does not require His exit from another room.

He is not fire. He *purifies* like fire.

He is not water. He *cleanses* like water.

He created humans (Job 33:4). He is the One who created the shape of all the animals (Job 26:13).

He is called the Spirit of *Life.* He is called the Spirit of *Peace.* Ephesians 1:17 calls Him the Spirit of *Wisdom.*

**102 What Is Deciding Your Present Income?** I cannot change your salary until I change the *problems* you solve! Every problem has a monetary value.

Does God decide who has money? If so, you would have to explain why the Mafia has it and missionaries do not.

Divine Laws decide the flow of money.

*When You Solve A Problem You Create Favor.*

Everywhere you find Favor, you will find money. Everywhere you find a problem solved, you will find Favor. *Favor Is The Currency For Money.* You cannot change your financial life until you change the problem you are willing to solve...for someone.

*Currents of Favor Begin To Flow The Moment You Solve A Problem For Someone* (WKMM# 115).

**103** **D**o **You Know The Reason Why We Enjoy Children So Much?** The two greatest pleasures on earth are finding someone you can trust and finding someone who trusts you. Why do we enjoy children so much? There is no distrust.

Trust is a gift.

*Trust Is The Seed For Safety.*

*Distrust Destroys Passion* (WKMM# 293).

I want God to enjoy me. When I wake up in the morning, I want God to look over at His angels and say, "He is up! He is up! He is up! Turn the blessing on!"

*The Proof of Love Is The Passion To Pleasure* (WKMM# 88).

*God's Only Pain Is To Be Doubted; God's Only Pleasure Is To Be Believed* (WKMM# 15).

**104** **T**he **Master Secret To Unending Favor In Life.** *Honor The Scriptural Chain of Authority.* It may be through your parents...the police...the Pastor...but the blessing comes down... through the Authority Structure.

The blessing does not flow upward.

It comes down through the Chain of Authority.

It was not someone under Joseph who promoted

him. His promotion came *through* the Chain of Authority.

I do not enjoy following laws. I have not found a human who inspires me to obedience. Not one! I have rebellion in every ounce of me.

I see a stop sign. I want to run it!

Rebellion comes natural to me. (I used to think it was because I was Irish. Now, I think it is just a human thing!)

The Chain of Authority is essential for your Financial Blessing. Read Lee Iacocca's book, *Straight Talk*. Read Donald Trump's book as he shares how he followed his father's Mentorship. Both show respect for the Chain of Authority.

Make a decision to follow and *honor* the Scriptural Chain of Authority. Remember how Isaac honored Abraham? Remember the reaction of the prodigal son to the Chain of Authority.

In the Ten Commandments, the fifth is the first out of the ten with a promise of a Reward. Are you in rebellion to any part of the Chain of Authority? It is critical that you go back and restore honor where due.

You may object, "Well, Mike, my father is not a Christian like yours. My daddy did not pray four hours a day...*six* hours a day."

Then, your Seed is even more significant...if you are willing to honor someone who refuses to honor you. Two Wisdom Keys are worthy to remember:

*What You Do First Determines What God Does Second* (WKMM# 224).

*Your Reaction To The Word of God Is A Picture of Your Respect For God* (WKMM# 71).

105 **Is It Really True God Is In Control...of** *Everything?* There is a teaching that should be evaluated again. It is the statement, "God is in control." If God is in control of everything that happens, then explain the 331 references in the Bible..."IF"... "IF"..."IF"..?

*Your Decisions Decide Your Future.* Not God.

Decisions decide who is comfortable with you and who withdraws from you. Success and failure are created by your decisions. "If ye be willing and obedient, ye shall eat the good of the land," (Isaiah 1:19).

If God controls everything that happens, what is His reward for Obedience? What is His reward for pursuing Wisdom? What is the penalty for rebellion?

God has not predestined your decisions.

God predestined the *consequences* of decisions.

*Champions Make Decisions That Create The Future They Desire; Losers Make Decisions That Create The Present They Desire* (WKMM# 342).

*Your Decisions Decide Your Wealth* (WKMM# 13).

106 **Your Mind Is Your Greatest Investment.** Invest in your Mind...continuously. It is more important than your family or your home. *What Happens In Your Mind Decides What Happens In Your World.*

If you are spending more money on your clothes than you are your Mind, you just want to look smart.

We spend more money on our car and wonder why it runs better than our brain.

Your Mind Is The Factory For Feelings. If it becomes troubled and distracted, it can destroy your work, productivity and relationships. Protect it with your life because it is very foundational to your joy.

**107** **The Master Secret To The Success of Abraham.** The secret of Abraham was more than productivity. He was a seeker of Peace. He avoided strife.

Strife *exhausts* you.

Strife *distracts* you.

*Strife Is The Proof Somebody Does Not Belong.*

Abraham discerned the Divine role…and the time-frame in relationships. He knew when the relationship was over. He also knew *how to exit the relationship gently.* Abraham knew the tragedy of ignoring the potential for strife.

Let me say something strong here. *Disrespect is concentrated information.* One moment of disrespect will show you more about somebody's character than ten years of relationship. Disrespect is a *signal* for more Dialog, Discipline or Disconnection.

*Anything Permitted Increases* (WKMM# 25).

**108** **Does God Have Favorites?** *God Does Not Treat Everybody The Same.*

Have you identified the top ten people who show you Favor?

"Mike, should I treat everybody the same?"

What fool would do that?

Jesus had seven *different* kinds of relationships. He acknowledged the Difference between Seekers and Critics. Yes, there is a profound difference in the people in your life.

For Jesus, there was a difference between the 12 Disciples, and the Inner Circle 3 and John, the Beloved. Jesus saw the difference between Israel…the Church… the World.

**Divine Rewards are different.** "I will reward every man according to his work."

God's reaction to us is different. Your pursuit of God is obvious to Him, meaningful and unleashes stored Favor. *Access Is First A Gift, Then A Test, Then A Reward* (WKMM# 47).

**109** **Y**ou Are One Instruction Away From Your Next Season. *Faith enters...and sometimes exits!* Faith is confidence...in God. Faith comes when you hear God talk. Faith comes when someone says what God said. It is sometimes affected by our pain or a third voice of doubt spoken into our life.

There are moments in your life when you will feel a stirring of...Uncommon Faith.

A famous lady teacher on television was telling me a few nights ago, "Mike, you do know how this Ministry got started?"

I had not. I had preached for her and her husband before they really started their church.

She explained. "I went to hear you preach. I had just been paid $200 by an orthodox church. It was all I had. You were playing the piano and you stopped in the middle of the piano playing and said, 'Somebody here is supposed to give $200, and it is all you have got. If you will sow it, God will bless you!'"

She said, "It was *everything* I had, but something leaped inside me and I sowed it. The next morning a woman walked up to me and said, 'God told me to give you $10,000.' The next morning, the woman came back and said, 'God told me to give you more. I am supposed to give you $5,000 more.' I took the $15,000 and launched my Ministry."

It was her Moment of Uncommon Faith! She

entered that Opportunity and unleashed a new world for her personal ministry. *Your Faith Decides Your Miracles* (WKMM# 329).

**110** **O**ne **Thing You Should Never Trust.** Your memory is faulty. Keep diaries and journals. Write notes continually throughout the day, or dictate into your digital recorder. *Never try to remember everything.*

If you could read insurance reports on car accidents, it would astound you to find what people remember...wrongly.

When I am training for leadership in my office, I insist that everything be written down...on paper or in their computers. Short pencils are better than long memories.

Use your mind for creativity...use a tablet or computer for storing what you want to remember.

*It will save you much embarrassment over tasks forgotten, neglected or done wrong.*

**111** **S**omeone **In Your Life Is Seeing Something You Are Not Seeing.** You need Right Voices speaking into your life, your heart... daily. Example: *A Mentor sees what you cannot see.*

Who is mentoring you? My father mentors me for *spiritual* matters, but not *financial* matters.

He gave me the Gift of *hearing* the Voice of The Spirit. Through that Gift, I was able to see and hear and feel God.

Whose Mentorship do you *invest* in?

Whose Mentorship do you *pursue?*

I bought some books some time ago at Books-A-Million. I spent over $900. I said, "Well I guess I am your best customer today."

They said, "You are our best customer *period.*"

I bought one little book for $84 and a young man with me said, "I cannot believe you paid $84 for one book."

I said, "Son, I did not just buy a book. What a man knows at 70, I will know in *two hours.*"

*Anything You Do Not Have Is Stored In Someone Near You, And Love Is The Secret Map To The Treasure* (WKMM# 102).

**112** **O**ne of The Keys To Discerning The Hidden Character of Others. *Reactions Reveal Character.* Reaction to Greatness...Change... Correction...a Personal Mistake.

Observe Reactions to Favor. When somebody shows you Favor, what is your reaction to it?

**Favor is a *Gift.*** It is a Harvest from a Seed. President George Bush, Sr. wrote his thank you notes in the driveway before he left people's houses after supper. The entire George Bush family is known to treasure every small sign of Favor.

*Honor* it.

*Celebrate* it.

*Protect* it.

*Maintain* it.

President George Bush, Sr. had 7,500 names on his Rolodex. Relationship is vital. Relationship is valuable. Whatever You Treasure Will Multiply In Your Life. Note well...those who trivialize your deposits and caring into their life.

*One Day of Favor Is Worth A Thousand Days of Labor* (WKMM# 39).

**113** **The Deception of Gray Hair.** Old men can do stupid things. Young men can do brilliant things. *Time is not a teacher.* Time has never been a teacher. Time will never be a teacher. That is why you have 80-year old sinners and 15-year old Christians...23-year old millionaires and 75-year old paupers. Gray hair does not make you smart. Neither does no hair.

*If Time Heals, God Is Unnecessary* (WKMM# 92). My Point: Listen well to all...but listen wisely.

**114** **Your Future Always Depends On Who Sees You.** *That is why The Presentation of yourself is important.* Very much so.

Think with me. *The king had to see Esther.*

Boaz had to *see* Ruth.

*People See What You Are Before They Hear What You Are* (WKMM# 240). The Wise discern the magical, miraculous and undeniable force, influence and power of...Presentation.

*How do you present yourself to others? In the presence of an Uncommon Leader?*

Access to a leader deserves a stricter Protocol.

Access Is Proof of Favor.

Continuous Favor Is Determined by Attitude, Adaptation and Presentation.

**115** **What Few People Know About Money.** Money is so incredible that God offers it as a reward for obedience. Think about that!

Psalm 112:1, 3, "...that delighteth greatly in His commandments. Wealth and riches shall be in his house." "...no good thing will He withhold from them that walk uprightly," (Psalm 84:11).

The Bible is full of reassurance that Wisdom produces wealth. Money does not go where it is needed. It goes where it is *respected*. You must develop an inner persuasion that money is a *weapon*. It is a *tool*.

*What You Respect, You Will Attract* (WKMM# 3).

**116** **N**ever **Stay Where There Is An Absence of Favor.** God talks through Favor. Naomi taught this Law to Ruth. Mordecai emphasized this to Queen Esther, encouraging her to talk directly to the king about the impending disaster being planned by Haman.

*Follow The Path of Favor.*

*The Path of Favor is the will of God.*

*God has not arranged any Success outside His will.* I consider *Favor* and *Peace* to be the two proofs of God's direction.

I went to buy a building one time. I made so many adaptations...so many concessions. The man was 90 something years old. He did not need any money. He did not care if he sold it or not. I was so worn out because I *wanted* the building so badly.

Finally, before I went to sign the papers for the last time, I went to The Secret Place.

I said, "Holy Spirit, I do not feel right about this. I want the building, but I do not feel right."

And He spoke and said, "There is no Favor. He has not made any concessions."

Adaptation is an investment, and this man would not adapt to anything I wanted or needed. And God helped me assess the *absence* of his Favor.

*Do not keep walking down a road where there is no Favor.* God uses Favor as a seal...as a *Verification* process. Favor is a *Confirmation.* Where do you see Favor?

*Honor* it!
*Treasure* it!
*Protect* it!
*Watch over* it!
*Pray over* it!

*Uncommon Obedience Unleashes Uncommon Favor* (WKMM# 211).

**117** **The Seed That Produced A Debt-Free Home...Worth Over One Million Dollars.** Seed-faith is the belief that you can sow a Seed toward a specific Harvest and God will honor it as a Covenant of Faith. Example: God had a Son, but He wanted a Family. He planted His Son on Calvary...and produced the Family of God..!

Few of us have learned this. It is important to always talk to your Seed...instruct your Seed...and speak aloud your faith for a desired Result from that Seed. *Your Seed Is Waiting For An Assignment!*

I was preaching for David Blount, a friend of mine pastoring in St. Louis, Missouri. I have known him since I was a teenage boy gr3owing up under my father's ministry. The Holy Spirit spoke to me, "Tell the church tonight that every person in the church should set aside a Seed equal to one month's mortgage payment and focus the Seed."

Because you must give every Seed an Assignment. You have to instruct your Seed *where* and *what* you want it to grow. Almost nobody does.

Take a moment to look back over the journey of your life...you will see a shocking thing...Seeds are wobbling all over the freeway of your past wondering

# Rhinoceros Facts

- There are five types of Rhinos...the Sumatran, Javan, Black, White and Indian.
- The Javan and Indian Rhinos have only one horn, and the Sumatran, Black and White Rhinos have two horns.
- Just like our fingernails, the Rhinos' horns are made of keratin and grow throughout their lifetime.
- Rhinos are about 60 inches tall at their shoulders.
- Rhinos live for 35 to 40 years.
- White Rhinos live in grasslands or open savannas with water holes, mud wallows and shade trees. Black Rhinos have various habitats, but mainly live in areas with dense, woody vegetation.
- Rhinos are vegetarians.
- Rhinos weight varies based on their type. Black Rhinos weigh 1 to 1 1/2 tons while white Rhinos weigh over 2 tons.
- Rhinos thick, hairless, gray hide looks indestructible, but their skin is actually quite sensitive, especially to sunburn and biting insects, which is why they like to wallow in mud.
- Rhinos have an odd-toed ungulate (three toes on each foot).
- Rhinos have large heads, broad chests and thick legs.
- Rhinos have poor eyesight...they are very nearsighted, which is probably why they will sometimes charge without apparent reason.
- Rhinos have a very good sense of smell and hearing.
- Rhinos have an extended "vocabulary" of growls, grunts, squeaks, snorts and bellows.
- When the Rhino attacks, he lowers his head, snorts, breaks into a gallop reaching speeds of 30 miles an hour, and gores or strikes powerful blows with its horns.
- Gestation period for Rhinos is 16 months.
- The closest Rhino relationship is between a female and her calf which lasts from 2 to 4 years.

where to go…what to do! You have never given them an Instruction. They are probably talking to each other, "What are you going to grow?" Another Seed responds, "I have no idea. He has never given me an instruction of where he wants the Harvest..!"

I went back about a year later…a young man followed me back to David Blount's office and said, "I have got to tell you something. I am living in a home worth $1.1 million. *It is now debt-free.* It is all because of you and that night you told us to sanctify a Seed equal to one month's mortgage payment…and focus it for the desired result of a Debt-Free house. "

He continued with a huge smile, "My home is now debt-free…because of your instruction to us to aim our Seed and target it for an Assignment."

Then he pulls out a $4,700 Seed check and said, "I saw another house on the lake I want to own now, too." I had to smile…as we had prayer together over the Harvest he desired for his second home.

*The Instruction You Follow Determines The Future You Create* (WKMM# 14).

**118** **What You Should Continually Test In Those Around You.** *Energy talks.* Enthusiasm is a picture of the heart. Always study what makes others excited…or what does not.

*Passion is intensity of desire.* Passion can be measured by the effort exerted to complete an instruction or obtain a specific goal.

Where there is no passion, there is no *creativity.*
*Where there is no passion, there is resistance.*
Passive people *resent* passionate people.

Passionate people are distracted in the presence of passive people.

One passive person can sabotage your dream.

*Laziness is the lack of interest in completing an instruction.* It is easily measurable and traceable by the lack of exertion of energy or effort.

Discern and identify those without passion... especially those you are allowing close to you.

Distinguish between those who appear passionate...from their actions that prove otherwise.

Some will use words...to divert your attention from their lack of interest and passivity.

Some use protocol as the tool of deception.

**In The World of Deception, Knowledge Is An Enemy.**

**119** **The Delusion About Money.** *Money Is A Magnifier of What You Are...*

A man drawled after service one night, "Well, Brother Mike, money can make you backslide."

I replied, "Then why doesn't the devil double your salary? When he went to destroy Job, he did not double his income, did he?"

Money is a *magnifier* of character.

Whatever you do with $10, you will do with $1,000.

What you do with $1, you would do with $100.

Money does not change you. *It makes you more of what you already are.*

If I give a gambler $10, he gambles $10.

If I give him $100, he gambles $100.

If I gave my mother $10, she would give it to the grandkids.

If I gave her $200, she would give it to the grandkids. (So, I stopped giving her money because she gave it to others. I started buying her gifts instead..!)

*Money Does Not Change You; It Magnifies What You Already Are* (WKMM# 140).

**120** **G**od Hides His Secrets In Very Ordinary Moments. God is a teacher. He uses Moments... as Carriers of Information.

*Moments contain Wisdom.*

*Moments contain Discovery.*

*Moments contain Secrets.*

It is your personal responsibility to discern the Divine Deposit of each moment...and extract the education planted there by The Holy Spirit...for you personally.

There are some people who are unhappy unless they are attacking someone. They can be in completely different parts of the world. Two different families. Two different directions. But one wants contention...

I cannot explain why some people pursue conflict...birth it...feed it...and are restless unless they are inside a battle with another.

But watching my ducks a few days ago...I saw this. Then, I saw my deer and antelope quietly graze next to the same ducks. No fight. No battle. No contention.

*Every moment of life is your School*...and the education you extract from it determines your ability to sustain your pleasure, your joy and your prosperity. Study every moment...for its divine distinction... difference...hidden deposit. The Present is as pregnant as your Future...with rewards.

*Joy Is The Divine Reward For Discerning The Divine Purpose of The Immediate Moment* (WKMM# 82).

**121** **H**umility Is The Seed For Promotion. Humility seeks...searches for change, improvement and even correction. The Non-Reacher has a Pride-Problem. Pride is easily recognized… through non-seeking.

*Those who do not seek…do not believe they lack. You Have No Right To Anything You Have Not Pursued* (WKMM# 237).

Humility is always…always…always rewarded… by promotion.

It is inevitable.

*It is eventual.*

*It is God-Decision Timing.*

Promotion is a *change* of responsibilities.

Any change of responsibilities involves *rewards.* God is very interested in His reward system for us and uses it as an incentive that unlocks our passion, energy and enthusiasm for change.

"Humble yourselves under the mighty hand of God, that He may exalt you in *due time,*" (1 Peter 5:6).

*The Proof of Humility Is The Willingness To Reach* (WKMM# 242). *The Willingness To Reach Births The Ability To Change* (WKMM# 45).

## 122 The One Sentence From Bill Gates That Changed My Life.

I read one sentence in Bill Gates' book when he was worth $87 billion. One sentence in his book, *Business at the Speed of Thought,* changed my life. *One sentence!*

Rule number three in Warren Buffet's book, *Five Laws of Investment,* would have saved me hundreds of thousands of dollars in my life.

Somebody *Knows* Something You Do Not Know.

Somebody *Sees* What You Do Not See.

Mentorship Is Learning Through The Pain of Somebody Else. *Mentorship Is Wisdom Without The Pain* (WKMM# 106). *Mentorship Is Success Without*

*The Waiting* (WKMM# 260).

Who is mentoring *you?*

Who are you interrogating *consistently?*

Who are the 3 most successful people you know and what have you asked them in the last 30 days?

**The Difference In Seasons Is Often A Single Sentence...You Choose To Believe.**

**123** **T**he Anointing That Excites You Infuriates Another. The Book of Acts is intriguing...fascinating and transforming. Especially the study of the varied anointing on the disciples... and the reaction of others to that anointing. *The Anointing Separates...even angers.*

When Stephen, filled with The Holy Spirit, began to proclaim truth...the crowd rushed on him. They stoned him. They killed him. Yet, others had been touched and changed by that same anointing.

*The same sun that melts the butter...hardens the clay.*

*The purpose of the Anointing is to reveal the character of others.* So, when God uses you in a spectacular way, do not be disturbed when some are incensed and infuriated. *Your Reactions Reveal Your Character* (WKMM# 276).

The Anointing is a Divider...a Plow...a Separator...and an Exposer of what is inside the hearts of men. Honor It...Protect It...and Sow It wisely into quality soil.

**124** **I** Will Never Forget One Night In Chicago. On a Wednesday night in a conference, a preacher got up and said, "How many would like to be debt-free?"

I smiled inside, because it dawned on me that anybody can be debt-free…in a day. Just let the car and house go back…to the creditors. Even the homeless are already debt-free!

And then he said, "Would you like to have a debt-free home?"

And of course, I said, "Yes!"

He said, "Plant a Seed *equal to one month's mortgage payment.* Write on the left-hand side of your Seed-Check Offering…*debt-free house in 12 months.* Hold it in your left hand and hit it three times."

I had never heard of such a thing in my life. Sounded a little weird! But, I knew he was a true man of God. I also remembered the Biblical account of the clay and spittle on the eyes of the blind man…very illogical, but Scriptural.

I did what the man of God instructed.

My house was debt-free in 8 months! Miraculously.

There will come a time in your life when God gives you a Moment of Uncommon Faith. Something stirs inside you!

*The Most Important Person In Your Life Is The Person Who Can Unlock Your Faith.*

With your Faith you can produce any Future you want.

It was a Moment of Uncommon Faith!

*Has God given you a Moment of Uncommon Faith and motivation to sow a significant Seed? Your Obedience…can forever change your Financial World.*

*Your Seed Is A Photograph of Your Faith* (WKMM# 287).

*An Uncommon Seed Always Creates An Uncommon Harvest* (WKMM# 14).

**125 Have You Identified Your Top 3 Agitations?** *Know yourself...well.* Identify Comfort Zones...and the Unhappy Situations where your weakness flourishes. Distinguish your personal needs...and what brings enthusiasm out of you. Everyone is agitated by different scenarios.

I have discovered that when I am rushed by others...I become angry, even when I have been waiting at length.

Examples:

A bellman is waiting at the door...for me to hurry and finish my packing, so he can take the luggage downstairs. That agitates me because I do not have the time I want to make a quality decision about where something goes...in the luggage. Knowing this agitation... I stopped calling a bellman up too early.

It agitates me to have to rush through an airport to the gate...to make it on time.

My solution: I go two hours early to the airport. It stops the agitation, the rush and simplifies everything. I can easily make the time count through using my laptop...reading...telephoning...returning telephone calls...or doing my Bible reading, etc.

My Point: Study What You Love...and make it happen.

**126 The One Sentence I Would Want You To Hear Before I Die.** If I were dying tonight and I had one sentence to tell you before I left...I would want one sentence engraved on your mind.

I cannot change your life until I change who you trust. *Your Future Is Decided By Who You Choose To Believe* (WKMM# 22).

This is well demonstrated from a book I read about

dogs...and their training. I love animals. I love dogs. I have studied dog training a lot. If you leave a puppy alone the first 12 weeks of its life it is almost unusable as a *protection* dog. A puppy that is left alone its first 12 weeks loses its *trust capability*. The fear capacity has developed in it so strong that it does not trust easily. It may be a great companion dog...run around dog...bark dog, but not a protection dog.

*Has your trust capability been damaged?*

Your salary is determined by the instruction you are capable of following.

Yes, even the Gift of Access is decided by the instruction you are capable of following.

*An Uncommon Future Requires An Uncommon Mentor* (WKMM# 338).

**127** **T**here Is One Place You Will Always Find **Money.** *Money is geographical. It is anywhere God wants you to be.* Money is only guaranteed by God at your Place of Assignment. Remember Elijah at the brook...and the Widow's house in 1 Kings 17? Divine instructions are always linked to financial provision. *Money Is Waiting For You At Your Place of Assignment...*

God designates your Assignment while you are in your mother's womb according to Jeremiah 1:8-12.

Your Assignment is always to a *person* or a *people.*

Your Assignment is *geographical.*

You do not belong everywhere. You belong *somewhere.*

*Money is the incentive for Obedience.* God continually presents Money as His reward for Obedience...to His laws. (Psalm 112:1-3.) When you honor a law, He rewards it with money. (Leviticus 26;

Deuteronomy 28.)

*Provision Is Only Guaranteed At The Place of Your Assignment* (WKMM# 136).

**128** **C**an A Bricklayer Become A Billionaire? The first time I ever heard Peter J. Daniels, the billionaire from Australia, within five minutes, I pulled out my credit card and gave it to my assistant and said, "Go buy one of everything he has got on his table."

Those who have what you do not have know something you do not know, *obviously.*

This guy was an illiterate bricklayer who could not read or write and got saved under Billy Graham. God touched him and he read 7,000 biographies.

I turned to my Travel Assistant and instructed, "Go buy one of everything he has got."

He came back and said, "He has got one that costs $750." He thought it was absurd that I would even think about buying books or videos so expensive.

I said, "I know, son, but still go ahead and purchase one of everything he has got."

He said, "Well, this one item only has two videos and a book and it still costs $750."

Patiently, I replied, "I know son, still, go ahead and buy one of everything he has got." *If your boss has to tell you something twice, he should get half of your salary.* I still believe that.

He resisted again, "If I buy one of everything he has got it is going to take $1,500."

"I know, son, buy one of everything he has got." You know it does not pay to be smart if you hire somebody stupid to travel with you.

Stubbornly, he retorted, "Do you think it is worth

$1,500?"

I stared at him stunned and said, *"Son, I am worth $1,500."*

*My Mind and Life Is Worth ANY Investment that unlocks my hidden greatness.*

**129** **The Person Most Qualified For Leadership Is The One Who Cares The Most.** *Caring qualifies you to lead others.*

You do not have to have a Ph.D. You do not have to be especially gifted.

The greatest quality for leadership is...truly caring about things being right.

*People Don't Always Remember What You Say, They Always Remember How They Felt When You Said It* (WKMM#186).

**130** **Are You Qualified To Receive The Universe God Wants To Give Away?**
One night, a single man was flipping through a catalog. He saw a woman with a beautiful gorgeous fur coat and it hit him. "Lord, I wish I had a wife to buy that for."

Then he saw a beautiful green necklace. "I wish I had a wife to buy that for."

Suddenly The Holy Spirit spoke to him. "Now you know how I feel."

He said, "I have got a whole universe that I want to give to somebody. All I am looking for is someone to trust Me. "

Knowing God...is the most important thing on earth. Understanding His nature...His heart...His desires for you is very important.

### MY PRAYER FOR YOU:

"Father, thank You for my precious friend and partner who is seeking Your Wisdom for their life, their family and for personal peace. Forgive us of any sin that has brought separation from You. Forgive us of any words that have planted pain, doubt or fear in the heart of others. Today, we reach for You...Your Grace...Your Wisdom...Your Plan for our Assignment. Breathe LIFE on our Garden...and cause these Words to grow the Fruit of Joy...the Fruit of Righteousness...and the Fruit of Prosperity. In Jesus' Name. Amen."

**Precious Friend:**

*I invite you to partner with me in the Gospel and the work of God. The Foundation of our Partnership is called...The Wisdom Key 3000. A powerful group of faithful believers who plant a Seed of $58 each month for World Missions and Evangelism. Will you become one of my partners today? Whatever The Holy Spirit speaks to your heart...will be a great blessing to so many. When you join, expect the 4 Harvests from Isaiah 58th chapter: Uncommon Health...Uncommon Wisdom...Uncommon Financial Favor and Uncommon Family Restoration and Reconciliation. When You Get Involved With God's Family...He Gets Involved With Your Family. I really believe that...and hope you will sit down and write me today..!*

Watch me LIVE every Sunday on the Internet by visiting our Website: WisdomOnline.com.

# Thank You

*...for Partnering With Me to spread the glorious Wisdom of God throughout the earth. I love the privilege of being your ambassador and personal intercessor. Please send your Prayer Requests to me and my Prayer Team at The J. E. Murdock Prayer Center.* The mailing address is: 4051 Denton Highway · Fort Worth, Texas 76117 · 1-817-838-PRAY (7729) · 1-817-759-0310 (fax).

# DR. MIKE MURDOCK

is in tremendous demand as one of the most dynamic speakers in America today.

More than 17,000 audiences in over 100 countries have attended his Schools of Wisdom and conferences. Hundreds of invitations come to him from churches, colleges and business corporations. He is a noted author of over 250 books, including the best sellers, *The Leadership Secrets of Jesus* and *Secrets of the Richest Man Who Ever Lived.* Thousands view his weekly television program, *Wisdom Keys with Mike Murdock.* Many attend his Schools of Wisdom that he hosts in many cities of America.

Unless otherwise indicated, all Scripture quotations are taken from the King James Version of the Bible.

*2 Minute Wisdom, Volume 4* · ISBN 1-56394-345-X/B-249/$7

Copyright © 2008 **MIKE MURDOCK**

All publishing rights belong exclusively to Wisdom International

Published by The Wisdom Center · 4051 Denton Hwy. · Ft. Worth, TX 76117

Publisher/Editor: Deborah Murdock Johnson

1-817-759-BOOK · 1-817-759-2665 · 1-817-759-0300

**You Will Love Our Website..! WisdomOnline.com**

**Accuracy Department: To our Friends and Partners...We welcome any comments on errors or misprints you find in our book...Email our department: AccuracyDept@thewisdomcenter.tv. Your aid in helping us excel is highly valued.**

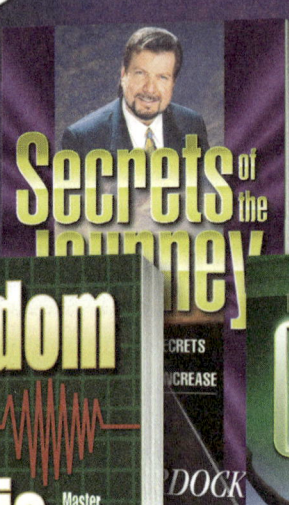
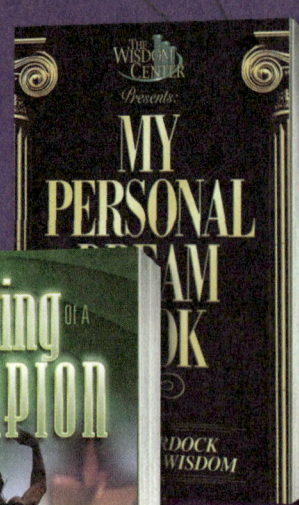
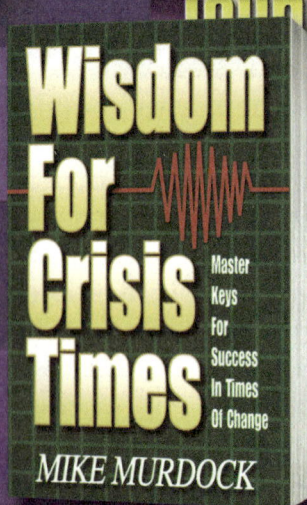
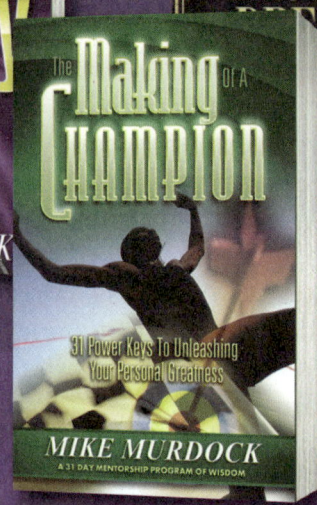

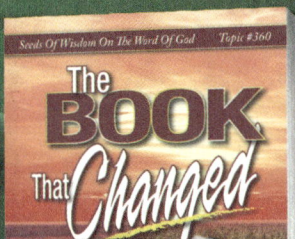

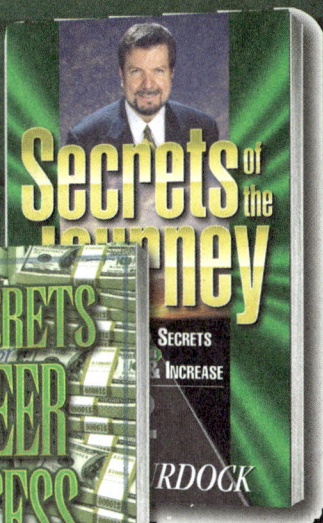

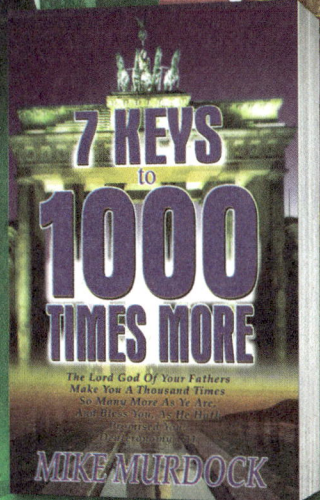

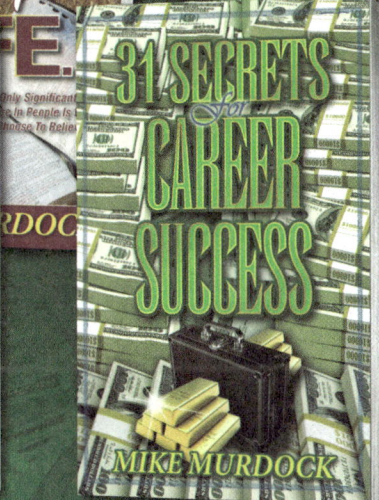

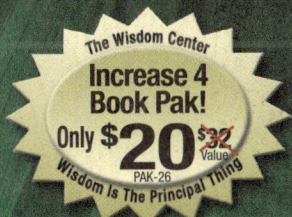

# GOD SECRETS 4
## Book Pak!

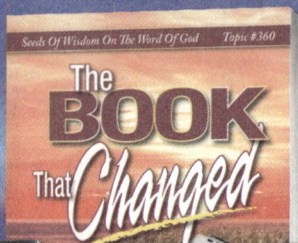
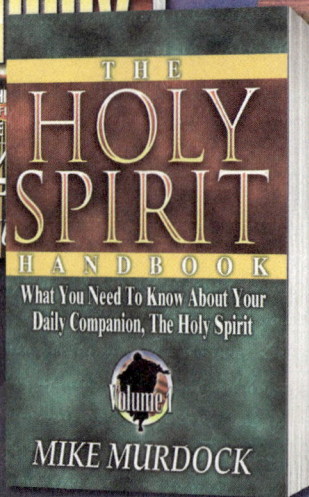
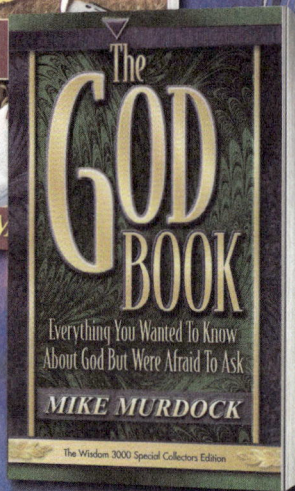

**❶ Secrets of The Journey, Vol. 4** (Book/B-95/32pg/$5)

**❷ The Book That Changed My Life...** (Book/B-117/32pg/$7)

**❸ The Holy Spirit Handbook**
(Book/B-100/153pg/$15)

**❹ The God Book** (Book/B-26/160pg/$10)

*Each Wisdom Book may be purchased separately if so desired.

Add 20% For S/H

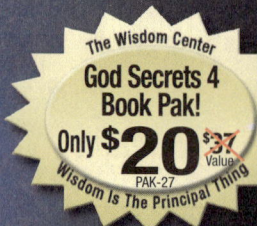

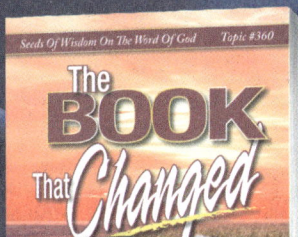

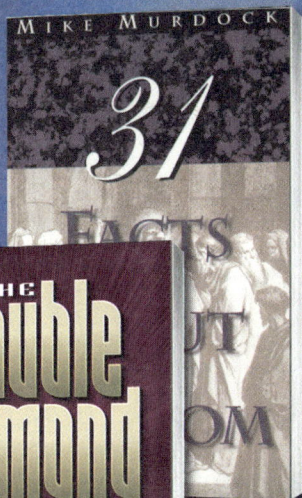

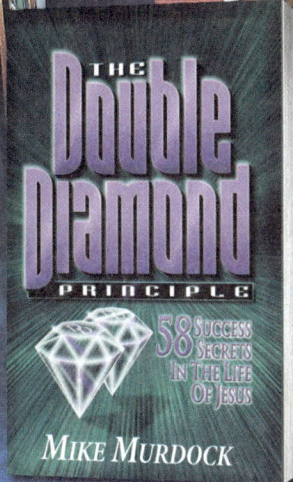

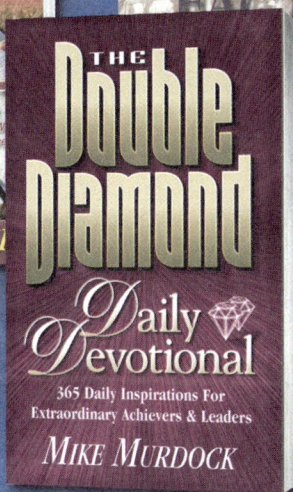

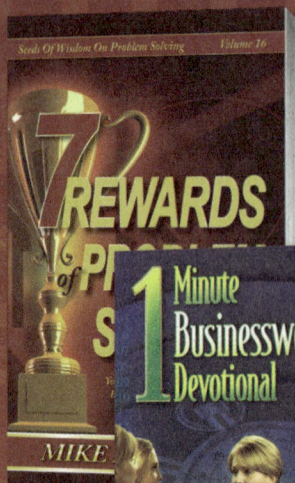

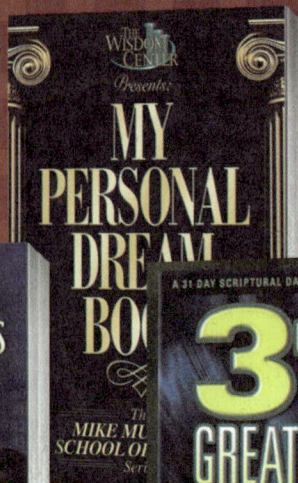

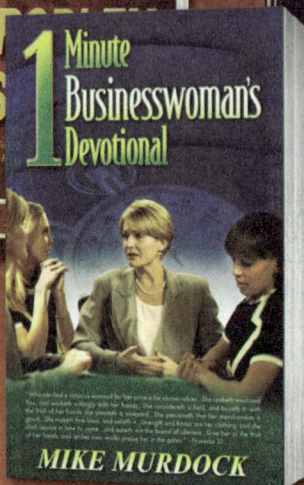

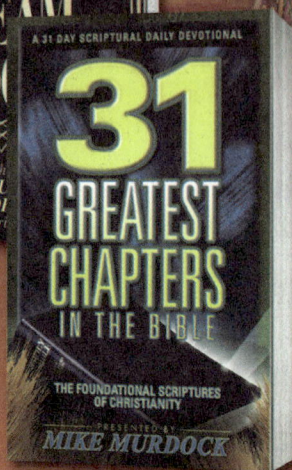